Contents

Introduction
'Down to Earth with
the Street Community'

'Down to Earth': Sharing about Jesus Christ in a way
that is easy to understand, inviting His Kingdom
'Down to Earth' in every situation, every day.

The word became flesh.[1] The Son of God chose to
give up Paradise for 33 years to befriend humankind
in person, especially Forgotten and Hidden people
like the Street Community (those rough sleeping and
those living in temporary or low-level
accommodation). Furthermore, despite being the King
of kings, He chose a life that was far from glamorous
where He never used His supernatural abilities to
bless Himself or make life easier for Himself. The fact
that it states in the Bible that Jesus did not have
anywhere to lay His head suggests that He was
homeless Himself, at least at times.[2] Jesus
understood and loved the Street Community.

I pray that this book and other things would help you
and me to understand, befriend and assist the Street
Community better. They are probably the biggest
group of Forgotten and Hidden people in the world
today. I recognise that this book is too simplistic at

---

[1] John 1: 1-18

[2] Matthew 8: 20

times but it is designed to give you a greater awareness of life for the Street Community, rather than a precise representation.

Chapter One
'Prioritising the Street Community'

Like most boys/men and maybe even most people, part of me desires to be a hero. With that in mind, I regularly try to be careful that I serve people out of wanting to help them for their sake rather than to fulfil this desire to be, or to feel like, a hero.

The pure part of my motives behind me helping people is that God has given me a GREAT love for all people, especially all of those who are forgotten and hidden in the world. Having this GREAT love made it very difficult for me to discern how I could help people to the max as I knew it was impossible to help everyone. After a while, God revealed to me that by devoting much of my time and focus to helping the Street Community, I would be able to serve a high number of people with a vast amount of needs.

By helping the Street Community, you help people facing rough sleeping and other poverty, addictions, mental illnesses, loneliness, low self-esteem, discrimination, spiritual imprisonment and even play a part in preventing trafficking and prostitution. In terms of what age bracket you are helping, you are generally helping people as young as teenagers up to people older than the UK retirement age!

If like me, you have a BIG heart to help the world and you do not know which group in need to focus on, I would suggest you help the Street Community to enable you to serve a diverse group of people with multiple needs. As you do this, ask God to confirm to you if this is the right focus for you. After all, it is not likely to do anything apart from a great deal of good, even if you just touch one life, for you to give helping the Street Community a try.

Chapter Two
'Just Like Everyone Else'

There are many false ideas about Rough Sleepers. Some label them as unintelligent, unpleasant and unclean.

Rough Sleepers are just like everyone else. Like the rest of the world, some are unintelligent, unpleasant and unclean and some are not. However, the countless Rough Sleepers that I have known since I was a teenager, have often been intelligent, pleasant and exceptionally clean, considering the circumstances that they are in! Furthermore, when they are sometimes unpleasant, I often remind myself of how unpleasant I would be if I had as little sleep as them and life as tough as many of them have it.

It is also sometimes assumed that Rough Sleepers are 'drunks', 'junkies' and 'ex-cons'. Some struggle with alcohol and other addictions and some used to be criminals, or even still commit crimes now, but they often have tragic stories that made it and make it very difficult for them to avoid bad choices. Furthermore, it is good to remind ourselves that Jesus said: 'Let any one of you who is without sin, be the first to throw a stone'.[3]

I greatly enjoy the company of most Rough Sleepers and most of the rest of the Street Community. In my experience, many of them are often far more genuine than many of those outside of the Street Community. It is an enormous privilege to sit on the concrete, being welcomed into a Rough Sleeper's space or to visit the humble homes that the rest of the Street Community live in.

---

[3] John 8: 7

Chapter Three
'Everyone's an Individual'

Just as it is dangerous to try and understand any individual by knowing their peers, we cannot understand a member of the Street Community because we have met others in the Street Community. Every person in the world is a complex individual and we cannot truly understand people without getting to know them as individuals.

If we want to assist someone in the Street Community, we need to take the time to hear their specific individual story and background, to help us identify their specific needs and then work out with them the specific resolutions for them.

Chapter Four
'No Way Out?'

Whether people are sleeping rough on the streets and elsewhere or living in low-level or temporary accommodation, it is so difficult for people to escape homelessness. There are a variety of reasons for this and as I said in the last chapter, you need to get to know each individual in the Street Community separately to really understand them and their circumstances.

Below are just some of the reasons for why it can be so difficult for many in the Street Community to find a way out of homelessness and unpleasant living.

Please note that a high number of the Street Community will be trapped in their difficult positions because of many of the reasons below, not just one of them.

- Having little or no finances.

- Having few or no family and friends to support them in any way.

- They are unable to have any accommodation of any kind because they are not entitled to this help as they are not from the area where they are applying so those from the area are given priority. Those from the area may have to wait a long time for accommodation if there is a sizeable waiting list.

- If they have success in getting work, it is very hard to maintain a job when you are barely sleeping and often have to walk everywhere that you go.

- Addictions, mental illnesses, or both, cause them to not be able to help themselves enough in the processes they need to go through to gain or stay in accommodation and those trying to help them can only do so much.

- Some have tried so hard for so long that they have given up on getting accommodation or better accommodation. With very little sleep and other struggles, it is hard for them to have the energy to keep trying.

- Some have waited so long for accommodation without any success that they have acclimatised to their situations. In some of these situations, they no longer desire accommodation even though it would be far better for them because the change would be too dramatic for them.

Through prayer, understanding each individual's circumstances and understanding the help available and unavailable to them, we can believe and work towards ways out for each member of the Street Community.

Chapter Five
'Scripture Screams!'

Scripture screams out for the poor![4] The poor are mentioned more than most groups of people in the Bible, and 'Poverty' is a regular topic that appears in numerous chapters. In the New International Version of the Bible, the word '*Homeless*' appears just once, '*Poverty*' appears 21 times and the word '*Poor*' appears 175 times!

It is worth noting that on some of the occasions that these words are used, the Bible is not referring to physical poverty but to spiritual poverty. However, the physical and the spiritual are related as I will explain in greater detail in the next chapter and I will also touch upon that subject now.

Remarkably, there are many Christians who are poor in terms of physical poverty but rich in spirit, sometimes even choosing to be poor or poorer than they could be, in order to bless others. However, sadly some people fall into spiritual poverty because of the effects of physical poverty. Either way, the

---

[4] Please note that the Bible verses used in this chapter and elsewhere in this book are all taken from the New International Version (apart from Isaiah 61:1).

spiritual and physical elements are interlinked and this goes for all things, not just poverty. We live in a physical yet spiritual world in physical yet spiritual bodies.

Another word related to poverty is of course '*Money*' which is a word that appears 111 times in the NIV Bible. My favourite Bible passage about money is Proverbs 30: 8-9:

'Keep falsehood and lies far from me; give me neither poverty nor riches, but give me only my daily bread. Otherwise, I may have too much and disown you and say, "Who is the Lord?" Or I may become poor and steal, and so dishonour the name of my God'.

This passage is wonderfully honest and identifies the importance of avoiding both physical and spiritual poverty. It is also interesting that the writer of the Proverb asks for '*daily bread*'. Jesus prayed and taught us to pray for our daily bread in what has since been known as 'The Lord's Prayer'.[5] This leads me to conclude that Jesus desires us to have enough that we will not be poor but not so much that we will be rich. Neither poverty nor wealth is likely to be good for the soul. Physical poverty will at least cause us to struggle physically, if not spiritually too and wealth is likely to make us too comfortable and cause us to not

---

[5] Matthew 6: 5-15

lean on Jesus enough, making us poor spiritually. After all, knowing Jesus increasingly is a treasure so rich that it makes worldly treasures look cheap. Let us now look at some other Bible passages about issues related to poverty and the poor.

Luke 6: 20-26

'Looking at his disciples, Jesus said: "Blessed are you who are poor, for yours is the kingdom of God. Blessed are you who hunger now, for you will be satisfied. Blessed are you who weep now, for you will laugh. Blessed are you when people hate you, when they exclude you and insult you and reject your name as evil, because of the Son of Man. "Rejoice in that day and leap for joy, because great is your reward in heaven. For that is how their ancestors treated the prophets. "But woe to you who are rich, for you have already received your comfort. Woe to you who are well fed now, for you will go hungry. Woe to you who laugh now, for you will mourn and weep. Woe to you when everyone speaks well of you, for that is how their ancestors treated the false prophets'.

These verses emphasise the superiority of spiritual wealth over physical wealth. As I said earlier, it seems that Jesus does not want us to be physically or spiritually poor but as these verses indicate, if someone has to face poverty, it is far better to be poor physically than poor in spirit.

2 Corinthians 8: 9

'For you know the grace of our Lord Jesus Christ, that though he was rich, yet for your sake he became poor, so that you through his poverty might become rich'.

This is how we become rich in spirit; by knowing and following Jesus who made Himself physically poor so that we could/can become spiritually rich. When we live our lives trusting that Jesus loves us, that He has paid for all of our sin, has won us a place in heaven and will never ask us to do something that we cannot do for as long as we are relying on Him, we will have everything. All our needs are met in Jesus.

Luke 12: 32-34

Jesus also said:

"Do not be afraid, little flock, for your Father has been pleased to give you the kingdom. Sell your possessions and give to the poor. Provide purses for yourselves that will not wear out, a treasure in heaven that will never fail, where no thief comes near and no moth destroys. For where your treasure is, there your heart will be also'.

We must give as our Lord Jesus directs us to give as unique individuals. How much and what He asks us to give to the poor and others will differ but all people are called to be <u>willing</u> to give up everything and anything. After all, He is the Son of God and He truly is all that we need.

Mark 12: 41-44

'Jesus sat down opposite the place where the offerings were put and watched the crowd putting their money into the temple treasury. Many rich people threw in large amounts. But a poor widow came and put in two very small copper coins, worth only a few cents. Calling his disciples to him, Jesus said, "Truly I tell you, this poor widow has put more into the treasury than all the others. They all gave out of their wealth; but she, out of her poverty, put in everything—all she had to live on."'

Whether we are physically rich or poor, this is one of many passages that show, with faith, we can all give generously.

Chapter Six
'Spiritual and Practical'

In our last chapter, we began to see how the 'Spiritual' and the 'Practical/Physical' cannot be separated. When we looked at Proverbs 30: 8-9, we saw a particularly clear example of how the 'Spiritual' and the 'Practical' are connected. In this chapter, I invite you to look more closely at this with me.

Jesus said for anyone who was thirsty to come to Him and drink and on another occasion that whoever drinks the water that He gives, will never thirst. In both instances, He is talking about the Holy Spirit. With all of that in mind, we can be confident that in one sense the 'Spiritual', specifically the 'Holy Spirit' is all that we need.[6]

When Jesus was in the desert for 40 days without food and to our knowledge without any practical or physical help, He proved that the Holy Spirit was enough to sustain us.[7] However, please note that the Holy Spirit led Jesus into the desert. Therefore, unless the Holy Spirit leads us into taking such steps into poverty, we should not put ourselves into that

---

[6] John 7: 37 and John 4: 14

[7] Matthew 4: 1-11

position. It is unwise to ever go anywhere where the Holy Spirit has not led us! This is one reason why it is good to pray for the Holy Spirit to help us know His voice better than any voice and to follow that voice wherever He leads us but nowhere that He does not. Furthermore, it is good to pray for Him to guide us with all decisions, including the thoughts we allow and do not allow to remain in our minds. Of course, we do not need to panic or obsess about any of this but it is helpful and for our benefit, as well as for His Glory, to live by the Spirit in these ways. As we attempt this, we need to remember to do this out of love and wisdom not fear or guilt, just like Jesus did. For it was for freedom, that Christ set us free![8]

In our last chapter, as we looked at the Proverb and remembered 'The Lord's Prayer', we saw that God is concerned about our physical/practical needs. I would suggest that no-one is likely to be led by the Spirit into a situation like Jesus was when He was led into the desert. I believe that it was a feat that only the Christ, the Messiah, our Saviour could face and accomplish. We are not called to be Jesus. However, we are called to be like Jesus and one part of that involves us allowing the Holy Spirit to enable us to do the impossible! I believe we will all be led at times to do something like Jesus' desert experience to an extent.

---

[8] Galatians 5: 1

Stephen Brunton, *Jesus Loves to Drive out Fear*.

The Bible teaches us to fast and the Holy Spirit will lead us into fasting in various ways, not just food and drink, that will push us out of our comfort zones. This strengthens our soul, helps us become more like Jesus and provides the opportunity for us to discover more of how the Holy Spirit is truly all that we need.[9] It is worth noting that if we choose to have a bad attitude about this or refuse to trust God, then it is unlikely to lead to such wonderful outcomes.

God's care for our physical/practical needs is spiritual as the Bible clearly teaches that the most spiritual thing is to love and we should follow God's example.[10] One Bible passage that clearly affirms these suggestions and our specific subject is James 2: 14-17. I will let those very verses speak for themselves to conclude this chapter.

'What good is it, my brothers and sisters, if someone claims to have faith but has no deeds? Can such faith save them? Suppose a brother or a sister is without clothes and daily food. If one of you says to them, "Go in peace; keep warm and well fed," but does nothing about their physical needs, what good is it? In the same way, faith by itself, if it is not accompanied by action, is dead'.

---

[9] Stephen Brunton, *Prayer is Action*.

[10] Mark 12: 30 and 1 Corinthians 13

Chapter Seven
'Spare Change'

To my knowledge, severe poverty exists in every country in the world! All poverty greatly saddens me but some situations completely break my heart. I will never forget when I was in Uganda in 2003 and I saw children walking around with pillows tied to their backs late at night. They looked about 5 or 6 years old and were walking up to cars driving past, attempting to sell the pillows, probably forced or instructed to by adults. At the time, I could not find the words to express my frustration and heartbreak for these children and others in severe poverty all across the world of all ages. 6 years later, I finally found the words that I wanted. They are written below. It is a simple song that I wrote in 2009 called 'Spare Change'.

Children begging on the streets, selling pillows so they can find a place to sleep.
We shut our eyes or watch TV, thinking 'If it bothers you, then it doesn't bother me'.

What have we become?
So overcome with selfishness and buried in our wickedness.
Why do we turn away?
If our children were suffering, would we respond the same?

Giving them nothing except for our spare change.
Oh Lord Jesus, how it must break Your heart.
Help us to at least pray for them each day.

And oh I can see You're moving!
Lord Jesus, You're fighting for them!
And if we would help them, we would see an end to their pain.
Yes, if WE would help them, we would see an end to their pain.

Chapter Eight
'Serving Suggestions'

I hope this book has been helpful to you and perhaps it has ignited a passion inside you to help the Street Community or another group in need.

On the next page there are some suggestions on how you could serve the Street Community. **PLEASE NOTE** that it is wise for you to get guidance from a homelessness charity or organisation before acting on some of these suggestions as it is good to do things appropriately and safely. I am confident that everyone can serve the Street Community in some way but before I make suggestions on how to do so, I just need to say...

We Need Them Too!

I have learnt and am ever learning more about myself, God, life and the universe because of the intelligence and goodness shown by many in the Street Community! Although, it is good for us to reach them with a servant heart, it is important not to patronise them. They have a lot to offer us too and the goal is to as appropriate, befriend them and to unite our non-Street Community with their Street Community. I hope for and aim for an end to all of this 'them and us' talk that we do. No more division! No more hostility! To become a 'family'!

OUR GOAL IS NOT JUST TO SERVE BUT TO HEAL THIS GREAT DIVIDE. WITH JESUS, THIS CAN BE ACHIEVED!

- Catering for the Street Community.

- Serving the SC food and/or drink.

- Listening to their stories and needs.

- Donating clothes of a condition that you would be happy to wear.

- Providing the SC something like the Street Sheet that the 'Off the Fence' charity that I work for produce. The Street Sheet informs the SC about many of the services that are available to help them with their various needs.

- Raising awareness.

- Where welcomed, praying for the SC and telling the SC about Jesus and the Bible.

In a nutshell, this is all showing and telling them about Jesus.[11] Isaiah 61: 1 is a beautiful summary of doing just that with the Street Community and the rest of the world. It is the perfect Bible verse and message to conclude this book with.

---

[11] Stephen Brunton, *Facing the Reality of Hell (A Call for All Christians to Evangelise)*.

Isaiah 61: 1

(See also: Luke 4: 18)

The Spirit of the Sovereign Lord is upon us because He has anointed us to preach Good News to the poor. He has sent us to heal the broken-hearted, to proclaim freedom to those captive and release from darkness for its prisoners.

Play your part in this incredible mission.

It is what you were made to do!

For King and Kingdom!

Our weapons are compassion, forgiveness, kindness, gentleness, boldness, perseverance, endurance, integrity, healing, grace, hope, peace and faith. In summary, our weapon is love and love will never fail.

#RaiseanArmy

Contact Information and Other Titles and Resources

If you have any questions about anything or you would like Stephen to preach, speak or lead a course at your church or group, you can contact him via downtoearthseries@outlook.com

Stephen Brunton's 'Down to Earth' Book Trilogy:

Volume One- Jesus Loves to Drive out Fear
Volume Two- Facing the Reality of Hell (A Call for All Christians to Evangelise)
Volume Three- Prayer is Action

Other Titles by Stephen Brunton:

The 'Down to Earth' Course Handbook
66 Deeper 'Down to Earth' Discussions
'Down to Earth' Worship Leading
'Is God Angry with me?'
'Should the Church Permit Baptism to a Practising Homosexual?'

All purchasable on www.amazon.com and www.amazon.co.uk

The 'Down to Earth' Course

In January 2016, Stephen began running the 'Down to Earth' course. An 11 week course designed for anyone interested in discussing life issues and the Christian faith in a down to earth manner and setting. For more information on the course you can contact Stephen and/or you can purchase the course handbook on www.amazon.com and www.amazon.co.uk

Stephen has used this and the '66 Deeper Down to Earth Discussions' book effectively at the 'Antifreeze' Homeless Day Centre that he manages in Hove, East Sussex, England to reach the Street Community with his team. Antifreeze is a segment of the 'Off the Fence' charity.

Course Structure

Week 1: Is there a God?

Week 2: Christianity and other Religions

Week 3: What is Sin and why would a Good God allow Bad things to happen?

Week 4: Miracles

Week 5: How does God view you? (The Cross)

Week 6: What does it mean to be a Christian?

Week 7: How can I avoid Sinning?

Week 8: Prayer and the Bible

Week 9: Who is the Holy Spirit and what does He do?

Week 10: The Importance of Churches and Close Friends

Week 11: Social Action and Evangelism

Printed in Great Britain
by Amazon

19456390R00020